The
STORY
of
Jesus

ELIZA R. SNOW

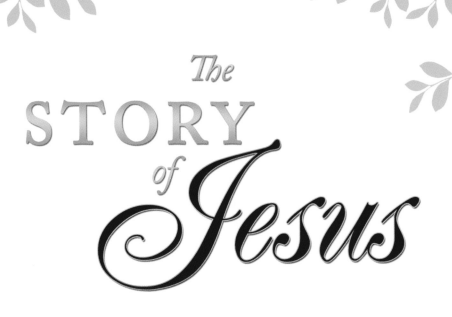

The STORY of Jesus

ELIZA R. SNOW

CFI
SPRINGVILLE, UTAH

Originally titled *The History of Jesus for Young People*, the text of this publication was written by Eliza R. Snow in 1867 and has now entered the public domain. The preface was written by Kathleen Barlow and may not be reproduced in any form whatsoever, whether by graphic, visual, electronic, film, microfilm, tape recording, or any other means, without prior written permission of the publisher, except in the case of brief passages embodied in critical reviews and articles.

ISBN 13: 978-1-59955-940-7

Published by CFI, an imprint of Cedar Fort, Inc., 2373 W. 700 S., Springville, UT, 84663
Distributed by Cedar Fort, Inc., www.cedarfort.com

LIBRARY OF CONGRESS CATALOGING-IN-PUBLICATION DATA

Snow, Eliza R. (Eliza Roxey), 1804-1887, author.
  The story of Jesus / Eliza R. Snow.
      p. cm.
  Summary: A history of the Life of Jesus Christ, written for children.
  "Originally titled The History of Jesus for Young People, the text of this publication was written by Eliza
R. Snow in 1867 and has now entered the public domain." -- t.p. verso.
  ISBN 978-1-59955-940-7
  1. Jesus Christ--Biography--Juvenile literature. 2. Christianity. I. Title.
  BT302.S66 2011
  232.9--dc23
                        2011018368

Cover art by Del Parson
Cover and page design by Megan Whittier
Cover design © 2011 by Lyle Mortimer
Edited by Grant S. White

Date of production: July 2011
Ages 4 and up

Printed and bound in China

10 9 8 7 6 5 4 3 2 1

Preface

The Story of Jesus was written by Eliza R. Snow in 1867 and originally published as *The History of Jesus*. Each chapter was printed one at a time periodically in volume two of the *Juvenile Instructor*.

Eliza R. Snow tells about the birth of Jesus, His ministry, the Crucifixion, and Jesus' many appearances to the Nephites after His Resurrection. Eliza R. Snow's comments throughout the story show that she and many other early Latter-day Saints had a great understanding of the gospel.

There were only three pictures in the original story, but they were indecipherable so I could not print them. The three pictures were of the Mount of Olives, the Garden of Gethsemane, and Jesus with the woman at the well. I also had to remove the three sentences referring to what the pictures were. Other than these minor changes and few other modernizations of punctuation, the text of this edition is printed exactly the same as the original.

The purpose of reprinting *The History of Jesus* was to make this story available in larger print, making it easier for children to read, so that the children in these latter days might get into the habit of studying the scriptures while they are young, and that they might read and know about the life of Jesus Christ, Our Savior.

—Kathleen Barlow

Chapter 1

JESUS is the Son of God. He is called, in the Bible, the Only Begotten, which means that He is the only Son that God has begotten in the flesh, on the earth, although God is the Father of all our spirits.

Mary, the mother of Jesus, was mortal just as we are, yet she was a pure and holy woman. In his parentage Jesus was unlike every other man, for, although he had a mortal mother, his Father was immortal, and thus he is God's only Son.

Thousands of years before Jesus was born, God had foretold his birth by the mouths of his prophets, and there were a few who had enough of the Spirit of God to understand what the prophets had said of his birth, and knew that the prediction was at hand. Nearly one thousand, eight hundred and sixty-seven years ago, Jesus was born in Bethlehem in Judea, on the continent of Asia.

It had been prophesied that he should be a great personage— he should be a Prince, a King and a Ruler over the nations of

the earth: and the great men of the world, who lived in that age, were excited to jealousy for fear that when he came he should take their power from them. They little thought that the mighty man, the Redeemer and Savior of the world, so much spoken of and so long anticipated, would come in such a humble manner; for he was born in a stable and cradled in a manger.

Not far from Bethlehem, at the time of his birth, some shepherds were watching their flocks of sheep, and an angel of the Lord appeared to them in the night, and the glory of God shone around them and they were afraid. And the angel said to them, "Fear not, for I bring you good tidings of great joy, which shall be to all people; for this day, in the city of David, a Savior is born, who is Christ the Lord." And the angel gave the shepherds a sign by which they might know who the child was. He told them where it was, and that they would find the babe lying in a manger, and just as the angel was going to depart, the shepherds saw a great multitude of angels, and heard them praising God and saying, "Glory to

God in the highest, and on the earth peace and good will to men." And when the angels had disappeared, the shepherds said one to another, "Let us go to Bethlehem and see if this thing which the Lord has shown to us is so." And they went and found Jesus lying in the manger as the angel had told them.

About the time of his birth, a singular star made its appearance, and some wise men in the East who read the words of the prophets, and were watching the signs of the times, knew that the star signified of the birth of Jesus, and they left their homes and went in search of him.

When Herod, who was then king over the land of Judea, saw the wise men, he inquired of them about Jesus, and wanted to know at what time the prophets said he should be born; and the wise men told him that they had seen his star in the east, and had come to worship him. And Herod commanded them, that when they had found the child, they should come and tell him, for he intended to destroy Jesus; although he told the men that he wanted to worship him.

And when the men departed from Herod, they saw the same star which had appeared to them in the east, and it came and stood directly over the place where Jesus was. And they were filled with great joy, and they went and found Jesus and Mary his mother, and they bowed down and worshipped him. And before they left, they gave to him very rich presents of gold and other substances that were highly valued in that country. But instead of going to that wicked king to tell him where Jesus was, they returned home by another way, for so the Lord had instructed them in a dream to do.

After the wise men were gone, the angel of the Lord appeared to Joseph (who was step-father to Jesus) and told him in a dream to take the young child and his mother and flee into Egypt, because Herod was seeking to destroy the child's life. And the angel told Joseph to stay in Egypt until he should be told to return. And they arose and departed in the night time, and did not return until after the death of Herod, that it might be fulfilled which was spoken by the prophet saying, "Out of Egypt have I called my son."

When Herod found that he had been mocked by the wise men, he was very angry, and sent forth a decree that all the children that were two years old and under that were in the land of Bethlehem should be destroyed, thinking by this measure to destroy Jesus.

After the death of Herod, Joseph was instructed in a dream to return to the land of Judea with Jesus and his mother, and they moved to the city of Nazareth, that the saying of the prophet might be fulfilled. "He shall be called a Nazarene." Once every year they took him to the Temple in Jerusalem. At one time, when he was quite small, a prophet by the name of Simeon who was in the Temple, took Jesus in his arms and gave thanks to God, who had revealed to him by His Holy Spirit that he should live until Jesus was born: and when he saw the fulfillment of the promise, he felt satisfied with life and said, "Lord, now let thou thy servant depart in peace, for mine eyes have beheld thy salvation—a light for the gentiles and the glory of thy people Israel." He prophesied many things that astonished Joseph and the mother of Jesus.

As Jesus grew in stature, he increased in wisdom much beyond his years; and when he was twelve years old, having been on the yearly visit to Jerusalem; his mother, thinking he was in the company; traveled a day's journey homeward, but when she sought for him and found that he was absent, she went back to Jerusalem and, after three days' search, found him in the Temple, sitting in the midst of the learned men and doctors, freely conversing with them—asking and answering questions. Those who heard him were astonished at his great understanding, but it need not have astonished them, had they realized that he was really the Son of God.

Chapter 2

JESUS was as singular in his character as he was in his parentage. His mission was very different from the mission of every other personage that has been born on this earth, for, in his mission he fulfilled the portion of scripture which says, "God so loved the world, that He gave His Only Begotten Son, that whosoever believeth on him should not perish, but might have eternal life." How strange! How very strange! But so it was—Jesus was born to die for man!

When but a small boy, the spirit of God, his Father, rested upon him and filled his heart with wisdom and his mind with knowledge and intelligence far beyond other children of his years; and this is what enabled him to converse with, and astonish the learned doctors in the temple, as was related in the first chapter.

Although Jesus was growing up to the size of man and was daily increasing in wisdom and understanding, he was very respectful and obedient to Mary, his mother, and to Joseph, whom most people thought to be the own father of Jesus. Jesus knew who his Father was, and yet it did not cause him to be vain or haughty; but he who was to be the Savior of the world, was a pattern of obedience and of all good and virtuous actions. He even went to a man whose name was John, who was baptizing people for the remission of sins in the river Jordan, and, although he had never committed sin, requested John to baptize him; but John, knowing that Jesus was the Son of God, felt a great degree of reverence and, feeling himself unworthy of the high honor, very modestly declined, saying to Jesus, "I have need to be baptized of thee, and comest thou to me?" But Jesus insisted that John should officiate in the sacred ordinance, that he might act an example for all people, and John consented.

A most grand and beautiful sight was seen at the time, for the heavens were opened and the Holy Ghost came upon Jesus and a dove came and lit upon his head as a sign that the Holy Ghost had descended upon him and that he was accepted of his Father in heaven, and a voice was heard saying, "This is my beloved Son, in whom I am well pleased." The voice was the voice of God, and the people who knew no better than to think that Jesus was the son of Joseph were greatly amazed, while those whose hearts were filled with the Spirit of God, which imparted understanding to their minds, rejoiced exceedingly and gave thanks to God.

It must have been a source of great comfort to Jesus, to have such a testimonial of his Father's approbation. But, as is frequently the case in the experience of good men, a trial awaited him after such a glorious manifestation.

Soon after his baptism, Jesus was led into the wilderness, where Satan, who is ever seeking to lead astray, tempted and tried to induce him to deviate from the path of rectitude and honor. Jesus had fasted for a long time—some say forty days, and he became hungry, and Satan very insultingly said to him, "If thou be the Son of God, command that this stone be made bread." But Jesus replied, "It is written, man shall not live by bread alone, but by every word of God." Then Satan took Jesus up into a high mountain, and in one moment showed him all the kingdoms of the world, and the glory of them, and told Jesus that if he would bow down and worship him, he would give him all, and at the same time, Satan was not owner of one of them. Then he took Jesus to Jerusalem, and placed him on one of the pinnacles of the temple, and told him to cast himself down from thence, saying, "It is written I will give my angels charge concerning thee."

These are good samples of the cunning arts of the Evil One, who is very apt in quoting scripture when it suits his purpose in prompting the Saints of God to do or say something that will darken the mind little by little and eventually lead to destruction.

But Jesus resisted all his temptations and would not yield to any of his falsehoods and, by resolutely struggling against him, got the victory so that he departed and after Satan was gone, holy angels came and administered to Jesus.

Chapter 3

JESUS loved little children. He often took them in his arms and blessed them, and he was heard to say, "Of such is the kingdom of heaven," and he told the people that if they wanted to please God and become members of His kingdom, they must be like little children. He meant good children— those that obeyed their parents and teachers, and did not use bad language nor tell falsehoods.

He taught the people that they should not be proud and haughty, and should not boast of what they did, and should not be idle; but they should be good and kind and always be doing something that was useful. Although Jesus was the Son of God, he visited the poor and the humble and spoke words of comfort to them, and told all the people who would listen to him what they must do to be saved from the evils of this world and hereafter be exalted to mansions of happiness, glory, and everlasting life. But many of the people in those days were wicked and loved wickedness, and many times when Jesus was trying to instruct and do them good, they would seek to kill him.

At one time, in the city of Nazareth where Jesus had lived, he was teaching the people in a house of worship, which by the Jews was called a synagogue, when a great many evil disposed persons joined together to contrive how they might destroy him, because he told them to forsake their sins and do right. They hated him whenever he reproved them for iniquity, just as wicked people do men of God in the present day; and they thrust him out of the synagogue and drove him out of the city to the top of the hill on which the city was built, intending to cast him down headlong; but the angels of God were around to guard and assist him, and he passed through the midst of the people and made his escape, and they had no power to hurt him.

Thus Jesus went from place to place, and when they persecuted him in one city he went to another; and he performed many miracles, in healing the sick and in rebuking and casting out evil spirits that had entered into people and were afflicting them. Sometimes the evil spirits would speak; for instance, when he was teaching in a synagogue in the city of Capernaum, there was a man possessed of an evil spirit, and it called out and said, "Let me alone; what have I to do with thee, thou Jesus of Nazareth? Art thou come to destroy me? I know thee, who thou art, the holy One of God." And Jesus commanded it to hold its peace and come out of the man; and the evil spirit cried with a loud voice and departed. And the people that saw it were very much astonished. After this Jesus went into a house where a woman was laying sick of a fever, and he took her by the hand and rebuked the disease and it left her immediately, and she arose from her bed and administered to the comfort of those present. Then they brought many to him that were sick of various diseases, and he laid his hands upon their heads and rebuked the diseases, and all were healed. And great multitudes flocked around him so that he had to rise very early in the morning to withdraw to quiet and solitary places to pray.

Perhaps some might think that a man like Jesus, who could perform such great miracles, would have no need for prayer, but he was a praying man, and was very careful to do the will of his Father in all things. What a lovely example for us to follow!

Jesus chose twelve Apostles from among those who believed on him—they were men whom he had called from their various occupations; several of them were fishermen—none were learned men, for those who thought themselves wise according to the wisdom of this world would not receive the pure and simple doctrine that Jesus taught and did not believe in him, for their hearts were not honest.

When Jesus had ordained the twelve Apostles, he sent them forth to preach and told them to go without purse and scrip; and he gave them power to do miracles and told them to heal the sick and cast out devils and raise the dead, wherever they found people that had faith to receive such blessings. And they went forth two and two, into the country of Judea, and wherever they went they preached, saying, "Repent, for the kingdom of heaven is at hand."

Chapter 4

AFTER Jesus had sent forth the Twelve Apostles to preach, he called others of his disciples by Seventies and sent them also.

The word disciple means scholar, student, or follower, and Jesus had many who followed him, some through curiosity to see the wonderful things that he performed and others to listen to his teachings and to treasure up the words of wisdom and kindness that flowed from his lips. He not only taught the things of eternal life but also taught them how to conduct themselves in all the relations of this life and even told them how they should be when invited to feasts—that they should not take the best seats they saw but wait till they were asked to go up higher. The Pharisees were too proud to teach people the most useful things; they were beneath their notice.

It was very strange in the eyes of the great ones that he who professed to be the Son of God should associate with common people and bless the poor and the humble, by healing the sick and in administering to their comfort; and many times great excitement prevailed throughout the country, and thousands of people gathered around Jesus.

One time he was in a desert place, and the multitude that came to him was very great, and [with] night approaching, his disciples requested him to send the people away that they might go to the villages and buy themselves food. But Jesus said they need not depart; and he told his disciples to bring him what food they had, which was only five loaves of bread and two fishes. He then commanded the people all to sit down on the grass, and, looking up to heaven, he blessed and brake the loaves and fishes, and gave to his disciples, and they to the multitude; and they all ate and were satisfied and took up twelve baskets full of fragments that remained. Those that had eaten were about five thousand men besides many women and children.

After that, he went into the land of Gennesaret; and when the men of that place knew of his coming, they sent into all the country and brought to him all that had diseases of any kind and besought him that they might only touch the hem of his garment; and as many as did so were perfectly healed.

There was to be a wedding in Cana of Gallilee, and Jesus, his mother, and a number of his disciples were invited to attend. Those who made the wedding feast failed of having sufficient wine to supply the guests during the entertainment. It would seem impossible that they should have been deceived in the number of their guests; for in that country, it was the custom for those who made weddings to provide and furnish every guest with a wedding garment, and no one could attend without being invited and not be discovered. But however it was, the wine gave out, and the mother of Jesus went to him, saying, "the wine is out." And she ordered the servants of the house to do whatever he required. He saw six water pots standing there, each holding two or three firkins (a firkin is nine gallons), and he told the servants to fill the water pots with water, and they did so. He then commanded them to draw out, and when they took the wine to the master of the feast, he pronounced it better than the other, saying the last is the best, not knowing how the servants obtained it.

Thus it was wherever Jesus went, if the people would receive him, he was constantly doing good, but alas! Many people, and nearly all who professed to be teachers—the Scribes and Pharisees—were too proud and too wicked to receive the truth, and they would not receive him as the Son of God, the Savior of the world; and, as strange as it may seem, they told all kinds of falsehoods about him, and sought, not only to lessen his influence with the people, but to destroy him.

And so it has been in every age of the world, and it is so now: when the Lord raises up prophets through whom He can speak and bless and save mankind from approaching calamities, those who profess to have the most knowledge are the most bitter persecutors. In the Bible, Jesus is frequently called the Son of man, which is an unmeaning expression through mistranslation. The name of God in the pure language is Ahman, and Jesus, in that language, is called Son Ahman, and from this the appellation of Son of man originated.

Chapter 5

JERUSALEM was a very grand and beautiful city. At one time, when a very great multitude of people had gathered around Jesus, he and his friends had a grand display as they entered the city amid the shouts of the people—Jesus riding on a colt and the people on foot.

When they were at a little distance from the city, Jesus sent two of his disciples to a little village not far distant, after telling them where they would find a colt tied, which they were to loose and bring to him, and if any one should ask why they were taking the colt, they were to say "the master has need of it." And the disciples went and found it as Jesus said; and when the owner of the colt saw what they were doing, he asked them why they did so: and the disciples answered the man as Jesus had instructed them, and he let them take it.

And when they brought the colt to Jesus, they spread some of their clothing on it, and then, after placing Jesus on it, many spread their clothes in the road, while others cut down branches of trees and strewed in the way. This was in fulfillment of the words of the prophet, saying, "Behold, thy king cometh unto thee, meek, and sitting upon a colt, the foal of an ass."

A great multitude of people went before, and another great multitude followed after, shouting with loud voices, "Hosanna, blessed be the King that cometh in the name of the Lord: peace in heaven and glory in the highest."

It was a joyful time for the friends of Jesus, and especially those who know him to be the Son of God; but the wicked priests and the proud Pharisees were very angry, and when they found that they could not silence the multitude, they went to Jesus and told him to stop their shouts and praises: but Jesus said to them, "If these should hold their peace, the stones would immediately cry out." Jesus knew the hearts of the wicked rulers, and often reproved them for their iniquity, and they hated him, and were continually seeking to find accusations against him, for they professed to be very righteous, and feared to have their wickedness exposed, lest they should lose their influence with the people.

As Jesus entered the city, he wept when he thought of the destruction that awaited it in consequence of the wickedness that was practiced in it, and he went into the temple and felt sadly grieved to see to what purposes they were applying it, for they had turned it into a place of merchandise instead of keeping it sacred and holy for the worship of God and the precious ordinances of His House.

And he cast out all those that bought and sold in the temple and overthrew the tables of the money exchangers and the seats of them that sold doves, and said to them, "It is written, my house shall be called the house of prayer, but ye have made it a den of thieves."

And the blind and the lame came to him in the temple, and he healed them.

When the priests and scribes saw the strange things that Jesus did, and when they heard the little children in the temple crying out Hosanna to the Son of David, they were much displeased and asked Jesus if he heard what they said: and Jesus said to them, "Yes, have you never read, Out of the mouth of babes and sucklings, thou hast perfected praise?" Jesus was delighted to hear the children shout and praise the Lord—he loved them because they were innocent, and their hearts were pure. God loves innocence and purity.

At one time, Jesus wished to retire from the multitude, and he went up onto a mountain, and a few of his disciples came to him: and he opened his mouth and taught them, saying;

Blessed are the poor in spirit; for theirs is the kingdom of heaven.

Blessed are they that mourn; for they shall be comforted.

Blessed are the meek; for they shall inherit the earth.

Blessed are they who hunger and thirst after righteousness; for they shall be filled.

Blessed are the merciful; for they shall obtain mercy.

Blessed are the pure in heart; for they shall see God.

Blessed are the peacemakers; for they shall be called the children of God.

Blessed are they who are persecuted for righteousness sake; for theirs is the kingdom of heaven.

Thus, year after year, Jesus spent his time in doing good to all who would receive good—those who were afflicted and had faith, he healed; and to those who believed his words, he taught the way of life and salvation.

Chapter 6

AS Jesus was traveling from place to place, he entered one of the cities of Samaria called Sychar. Some land was there which the ancient patriarch Jacob gave to his son Joseph. (The same Joseph who was sold into Egypt.) On that land was a well of water; it was called Jacob's well. And Jesus being weary with his journey, sat down on the side of the well, to rest: and while he sat resting himself, the woman came to draw water, and Jesus asked her to give him a drink, for his disciples had all gone to the city to buy food, and Jesus was left alone.

It was very unusual for Jesus to be alone, for he was so different and taught so differently from the professed teachers in Israel, that he attracted so much attention, that when he wanted retirement, he had to go away into distant places to get from the multitudes of people that continually flocked around him.

What an honor it was to that woman of Samaria, to have the privilege of administering to Jesus a drink of water. But she was just as ignorant as many people are now, when the servants and prophets of God are in their midst and they do not know it. She did not know Jesus, nor think that he was the Son of God, or she would not have answered him as she did, by asking him how it was that he being a Jew should ask drink of a Samaritan; for at that time, the Jews had no dealings with the Samaritans. Jesus told her that if she had known the gift of God and who it was that said, "Give me to drink," she would have asked of him, and he would have given her living water.

The woman did not understand him—she did not know what he meant by the gift of God and living water, and she replied by saying that the well was deep, and he had nothing to draw with, and wanted him to tell her how he could get the living water. She said to him, "Art thou greater than our father Jacob, who gave us the well and drank of it himself, his children, and his cattle?" Jesus then said to her, "He that drinks of this water will thirst again; but he that drinks of the water that I shall give shall never thirst, but the water that I shall give him shall be in him a well of water, springing up into everlasting life." Jesus then told the woman to go and call her husband. He knew that she had no husband, but he wanted to prove her whether she would tell the truth. She told him that she had none; and then he said to her that she had truly spoken, for she had five, and the one she lived with then was not her husband. She then began to think he was a prophet and listened attentively to him while he instructed her how God should be worshipped in spirit and in truth and told her that he was the Savior of whom the prophets had spoken. And she left her water pot and went into the city and told the people to come and see a man that told her all things that she ever did, and many came out to see him and believe on him.

Before Jesus was done talking with the woman, his disciples returned from the city and thought very strange and wondered among themselves that he talked with her but did not question him on the subject. He had told those who thought themselves wise that the publicans and harlots would go into the kingdom of God before them. Jesus came to save those that were lost by teaching them to repent and forsake sin and live righteous and holy lives. It did not matter with him whether they were rich or poor—high or low—noble or ignoble—good or bad, if they would forsake every thing that was evil, be baptized for the remission of their sins, and then live by every word that is spoken by the mouth of God.

It is much easier for those who are properly taught when they are small children, and learn when they are young, to do right than it is for those who have indulged in bad habits; and yet, no one should feel discouraged, for Jesus did not, and will not, reject any that will strive to keep his commandments.

From Sychar, Jesus went again into Cana of Galilee, the place where he attended a wedding feast some time before, and turned water into wine. A nobleman was there who had a son lying very sick at Capernaum; and he found Jesus and entreated him to go and heal his son. Jesus said to the man, "Except you see signs and wonders, you will not believe." But the man was afraid the child would die and kept urging him

to go immediately. And Jesus said to him, "Go your way, your son lives." The man believed the word and went his way; and as he was going, his servants met him and said, "Thy son lives." And he inquired and found that he began to recover at the same time that Jesus said to him, "Thy son lives." And the nobleman and his whole family believed.

Chapter 7

JESUS came on the earth to die; it was a part of his mission; for, as it is written, "God so loved the world that he gave His Only Begotten Son to die for the sins of the world."

It was a very hard thing for his apostles to believe that Jesus would be put to death, for they had been so much with him, they knew him to be good and innocent. From time to time, he would intimate to them, and tried to make them understand that the enemies of truth would take his life, and even told them that he would be betrayed into their hands.

As Jesus sat in the house of his friends, in a place called Bethany, a woman came in with a box of very precious and costly ointment and poured the ointment on his head. Judas, one of the twelve, was much displeased and found fault with the woman because she had wasted the precious ointment and said, "Why was not this ointment sold for three hundred pence and given to the poor?" He did not ask this question because he cared for the poor, but he was dishonest, and, as he was the treasurer and took charge of the money, he would get possession of it and put it in his own pocket. We shall see what becomes of Judas. No dishonest person will prosper for a great length of time. They may seem to do so for a season, but God is sure to reward them according to their works, and they will sooner or later come to a bad end. None but honest people will remain in the kingdom of God.

Jesus told Judas to let the woman alone, for she had done right—she had anointed him for his burial. And he said to his apostles that they always had the poor with them and always had opportunities for doing them good, but they would not always have him, and he said that what the woman had done should be told in remembrance of her, wherever the gospel was preached, till the end of the world.

Once every year, the people called Jews were required to go up to Jerusalem to keep the feast of the Passover from the circumstance of the Israelites passing over the Red Sea when the Lord delivered them from the cruel bondage of Pharaoh, the king of Egypt. It was a marvelous deliverance, for the Lord divided the water of the sea so that Moses led the people through on the bottom of the sea, while the water was rolled up like mountains on each side of them; but Pharaoh and all his army, who followed the Israelites to destroy them, were drowned in the sea, for the Lord let the water roll back again into the bed of the sea and buried them. Then the Lord commanded the Israelites to celebrate that day and keep it in remembrance by making a feast of unleavened bread every year on the same day of their great deliverance.

Jesus and his apostles went up to Jerusalem to keep this feast, in which they were not allowed to eat any light bread, and it was sometimes called the feast of unleavened bread. On the evening of the first day of the feast, Jesus sat down to supper with his Twelve Apostles, and as they were eating, he said that one of them would betray him. This made them feel very sorrowful, for they knew that wicked men who held the authority were seeking to find some pretence against him so that they might take him, and each one said to him, "Lord, is it I?" Jesus knew who it was, and he told them how they might know, for he said the one who would betray him would dip in the same dish with him. And he said, "Woe to that man by whom the Son Ahman is betrayed! It would have been well for that man if he had never been born."

Then Jesus took bread and blest and brake it and gave to them, and said, "Take, eat; this is my body." And he took the cup and blest it in the same manner, and told them all to drink of it and said, "This is my blood of the New Testament, which is shed for many; verily, I say unto you, I will drink no more of the vine until I drink it new in my Father's kingdom." This is what is called the Lord's Supper, it being the last he partook of before his death, and he commanded his disciples to do the same, in remembrance of him, until he comes again on the earth in the last days. This is why the Latter-day Saints partake of the sacrament—*sacrament* means the same as the Lord's Supper. And when they had sung a hymn, they went out into the Mount of Olives. They called it a Sabbath day's journey (three miles) from Jerusalem. On this Mount, Jesus sat when he told Peter that before the cock should crow twice,

he would deny Jesus three times, but Peter could not believe it. He said if he should die, he would not deny Jesus. But Peter did not know what he would do, for in that respect, he had not been tried.

Chapter 8

IN the garden of Gethsemane, Jesus retired with three of his apostles, Peter, James, and John.

He knew that the time was approaching when not only all men would forsake him, but when the great God, his Father, would so far withdraw His power and protection from him that his enemies would prevail over him and take his life in a most cruel and disgraceful manner. He who was to be a sacrifice for the world seemed, at that time, to feel the weight of the sins of the whole world resting upon him.

He was pure and innocent, and in this respect, his feelings were very different from those of a wicked person, for nothing is so hard to bear as a feeling of guilt. Jesus knew he was to die a cruel death—he had consented to redeem the world. Long before the earth existed, he had even volunteered to do it when he dwelt with his Father, at the time when the great plan of man's redemption was formed in the midst of a grand council of the Gods. And Jesus had a very keen and painful foretaste of the dreadful scene of suffering that awaited him; and he told the three apostles who were with him in the garden of Gethsemane that his soul was exceedingly sorrowful, and he desired them to remain where they were and keep watch while he went a short distance to pray. He went and fell on his face and prayed: "O Father, if it is possible, let this cup pass from me, nevertheless, not as I will, but as thou wilt."

How strange it was, that in such a time of anguish of mind which Jesus was passing through, that those apostles should have been so destitute of sympathy as to suffer themselves to fall asleep when he had requested them to watch! But the powers of darkness were so great that when Jesus returned to them, he found them fast asleep and said, "What! Could you not watch with me one hour?" He saw they had no control over themselves and excused them by saying, "Truly, the spirit is willing but the flesh is weak." He then went from them the second and third time and prayed the same as at the first; and his agony of feeling was so great that, instead of perspiring as people naturally do, his sweat was in large drops, like blood.

Each time when he returned to Peter, James, and John, he found them asleep, and the last time, he told them to sleep on and take their rest, for the hour was near when the Son Ahman should be betrayed into the hands of sinners. He then said to the three apostles, "Rise, let us be going. He that betrays me is at hand." And before Jesus had done speaking, Judas, one of the Twelve Apostles, and a great multitude came with swords to take him. This multitude was nothing more nor less than a mob with an Apostle at their head, and they were urged on to this wickedness by the chief priests and elders of the people. The Latter-day Saints, who have been in this church nearly from its commencement, have had considerable experience in movements very similar to the one described; for the multitude that went to take Jesus were so ignorant of him that Judas had to give them a sign that they might know which was the one to take—they did not even know his person, but Judas told them that whosoever he should kiss they were to grasp and hold fast; and when he came to Jesus, he said, "Hail, master," and

kissed him. Jesus said to him, "Judas, betrayest thou the Son Ahman with a kiss?"

One that was a friend to Jesus felt so indignant at seeing them lay hands on him that he drew his sword and struck a servant of one of the high priests and cut off his ear. But Jesus reproved him by saying, "Put your sword back in its sheath; for all they that take the sword shall perish by the sword." He then put forth his hand and healed the wounded man and said to the one that smote him, "Think you that I cannot now pray to my Father, and He shall immediately send me more than twelve legions of angels? But how, then, shall the scriptures be fulfilled, that thus it must be?"

Not long after they had taken him, Jesus said to some of the multitude, "Are ye come out as against a thief, with swords and staves, to take me? I sat daily with you in the temple, teaching, and you did not lay hold of me." But all this was done that the words of the prophet might be fulfilled.

Then all of the Apostles forsook Jesus, and fled, and left him in the midst of his enemies, who took him to a high priest called Caiaphas, where many priests and scribes had assembled; but Peter followed in the distance and went into the high priest's palace and sat with the servants to see the result. And he heard those wicked priests and elders counseling together, trying to find some accusation against Jesus so that they could put him to death; but they could not find any. At last there came two false witnesses who testified that he said he was able to destroy the temple of God and build it in three days, and that was the worst that even false witnesses dare to say against him. Jesus made no reply, although the high priest was very anxious that he should, that from his replies, they might get something to accuse him of. Jesus knew their thoughts, and when the high priest found that he could not persuade Jesus to answer the false witnesses, he said, "I entreat you by the living God, to tell us whether thou art the Christ, the Son of God." Jesus then said to him, "Thou hast said, and I say to you that hereafter, you shall see the Son Ahman sitting on the right hand of power, and coming in the clouds of heaven."

Chapter 9

THESE are sad events in the history of Jesus. After what he had said, as related in the preceding chapter, the high priest then rent his clothes and accused Jesus of having spoken blasphemy and asked the people what need there was of any witness against him, as they had heard his blasphemy, and said, "What think you?" They said, "He is guilty of death." They then spit in Jesus's face, and some struck him with their hands, and, having covered his face, they ridiculed him by telling him to prophesy and tell them who it was that struck him.

All this time Peter was in the palace, sitting with the servants, and one of the servant girls said to him, "You were with Jesus of Galilee," but he denied it before all that were present, and then the cock crowed. But Peter took no notice of it and went out into the porch, where another young woman knew him and said to some that were standing by, "This fellow was with Jesus," and this time he denied it with an oath and said he did not even know the man. Then after a little while, those that stood by said to him, "Surely you are one that was with Jesus, for your speech betrays you." Then Peter began to curse and swear and said again that he did not know the man; and immediately the cock crew the second time, and Peter remembered the words of Jesus, "Before the cock crows twice, thou shalt thrice deny me," and he went out and wept bitterly.

The next morning all the chief priests and leaders of the people took counsel against Jesus to put him to death; and they bound him and led him away and delivered him to the governor, whose name was Pontius Pilate. And Jesus stood before the governor, who asked him if he was the king of the Jews. Jesus replied, "You have said it."

Then Pilate, after he had examined Jesus, said to the priests and to the people, "I find no fault in this man." When they saw that the governor felt disposed to justify Jesus, they were more fierce and clamorous against him and accused him of making disturbances among the people and of teaching them to be disloyal to Caesar, the Roman emperor who held jurisdiction over the inhabitants of Judea, and had appointed Pilate, who was not a Jew, to be a governor in Jerusalem.

It will be recollected that Jesus and his Twelve Apostles had come up to Jerusalem to keep the feast of the Passover. At this feast it was customary to release a criminal—that is, to let one of the prisoners go free from prison. And Pilate, thinking that Jesus was innocent, tried to persuade the people to let him release Jesus unto them, but, as the people had the privilege of deciding which one should be set at liberty, he could not make the choice without their consent. There was one noted prisoner who had committed murder as well as other crimes, and they told the governor to release him and crucify Jesus, although the governor continued to declare his innocence, for he knew that it was through envy that they wished to destroy him. While Pilate was sitting on the judgment seat, his wife entered the judgment hall and told him not to do any thing with that just man, for she had been warned in a dream. But the priests were very busy with the people in urging them to ask for the murderer, whose name was Barrabbas, to be released; and Pilate asked them what he should do with Jesus. And they all cried out, "Let him be crucified." Pilate said, "Why, what evil hath he done?" But they cried out, "Let him be crucified." When Pilate saw that he could not prevail and that they were getting tumultuous, he took water and washed his hands in the sight of the multitude and said, "I am innocent of the blood of this just person—see you to it. I have found no cause of death in him." Then all the people answered and said, "His blood be upon us and on our children." And the curse of God has rested upon the Jews from that day to this—they have never prospered as a nation—the beautiful city of Jerusalem has been destroyed, and they have been, and are still, scattered among all nations; but according to the predictions of the ancient prophets, the time is near when they will return to the land of Judea and rebuild the city of Jerusalem. The Jews are proverbially lovers of money, and some of the largest capitalists in Europe are Jews. Jesus was betrayed for money; Judas received thirty pieces of silver for betraying Jesus to his enemies. But the money did him no good—he got it wickedly,

and his guilty conscience gave him no peace, for as soon as he saw that Jesus was condemned, he was sorry for what he had done, and he brought the thirty pieces of silver back to the chief priest of whom he had received it, saying, "I have sinned in betraying innocent blood." They said to him, "What is that to us?" Judas threw the money down in the temple and went out and died an ignominious death, such as a traitor merits. No character is more despicable than that of a traitor, and no death was considered so disgraceful by the Jews as hanging. It is said of Judas that he hung himself.

Chapter 10

JESUS came upon the earth in a time when those who administered in the government were so corrupt that justice could not be administered. In this respect, it very much resembled the day in which we live. It did not matter how good the laws were when those who stood in high places were too selfish to see them executed with justice. A ruler, who has not influence sufficient to defend the innocent, is a ruler only in name. Pilate felt that Jesus was innocent, and he should have scorned the office of governor when he found that he had not power enough in the midst of the people, to protect him. He disgraced his position when he delivered Jesus into the hands of his enemies—he had better have died in the noble discharge of his duty than so meanly to have yielded his judgment, but he stood alone—opposed by the whole multitude of priests, judges, and people.

After the soldiers got Jesus into their hands, they treated him with all kinds of abuse. They took off his clothes, dressed

him in a purple robe, and plaited a crown of thorns which they placed on his head, and put a reed in his right hand, and then made all manner of ridicule. Pretending to worship him, they bowed their knees before him, and in cruel mockery, they said, "Hail, King of the Jews!" Then they spit in his face and struck him with their hands. After they had gratified their hellish feelings in this way till they were satisfied, they took off the purple robe and dressed him again in his own clothing. Purple was then, in the East, the royal color and worn only by kings and princes, and it was in derision that the soldiers put it on Jesus; and when they had taken the robe off and put on his own clothes, they led him away to crucify him, which means to nail to a cross. They had the cross on which they intended to hang Jesus already made, and, at first, they compelled him to carry it, but afterwards they found a man from the country, whom they required to carry it for him. They took him to a place called Golgotha, which signifies "The place of a skull," and made him fast by driving a nail through each hand and foot and thus nailing him to the cross, which was made of wood.

This is the way the wicked Jews crucified Jesus Christ, the Son of God, the Savior of the world! What excruciating sufferings he must have endured in that dreadful position, while those that passed by ridiculed and insulted him in the most shameful manner possible, saying, "Save thyself and come down from the cross, thou who canst destroy the temple and build it in three days. If thou art the Son of God, come down from the cross, and we will believe on thee." And the chief priests and scribes, mocking him, said, "He professes to save others, but he cannot save himself. Let Christ, the king of Israel, descend from the cross."

There were two thieves crucified with Jesus. One of them reproached Jesus by saying, "If you are what you profess to be, save yourself and us." But the other one reproved him and asked him if he did not fear God, seeing he was under condemnation, for they were receiving the just punishment for their crimes while Jesus had done no wrong. Then he

said to Jesus, "Lord, remember me when thou comest into thy kingdom." Jesus replied, "Today you shall be with me in Paradise." Paradise signified then the world of spirits, or the place to which all spirits go when they leave this life. The ancient Greeks called it Hados.

Many people who were friends of Jesus followed in the distance, and many mingled silently in the crowd, and while their hearts were ready to break with grief, they were not allowed even the privilege of speaking with him. A striking proof of the kindness of his compassionate heart was illustrated while in that state of agonizing suffering: Jesus, seeing his mother standing by the cross and one of his Apostles whom he dearly loved, said to his mother, "Behold your son," and to the Apostle he said, "Behold your mother." The Apostle, whose name was John, understood at once what Jesus wanted, and he took his mother home with him and provided for her comfort as long as she lived.

During all his dreadful suffering, Jesus did not utter one word of complaint but even prayed for his murderers by saying, "Father, forgive them, for they know not what they do." Seeing women who had followed to the place weeping, he said to them, "Daughters of Jerusalem, weep not for me, but weep for yourselves and your children."

Pilate, the governor, wrote an inscription in the Greek, Latin, and Hebrew languages, and had it placed on the cross over the head of Jesus. THIS IS THE KING OF THE JEWS.

Three hours Jesus hung upon the cross in agony—he asked for drink, and one of the soldiers brought some vinegar mixed with gall, which he tasted but did not drink. He then said, "Father, I have finished the work thou gavest me to do; into thy hands I commend my spirit." And having said this he breathed his last. And then was darkness over all that land—the sun was darkened—the rocks were rent asunder. The veil of the temple also was rent, and all nature mourned. Many of those who came out to see were convinced of the mighty power of God and acknowledged Jesus to be His Son, while fear and astonishment filled the hearts of the ignorant, wicked multitude.

Chapter 11

WE can better imagine than describe the feelings of the Apostles and friends of Jesus when they saw him expire on the cross. If they had understood his sayings, they would have found comfort in hope of his resurrection; but they had not comprehended them, and his death was, to them, the end of all their hopes and anticipations, and instead of triumphing over those who had opposed them, they were subject to all the scorn and ridicule that their enemies could heap upon them.

Jesus was crucified on Friday. Saturday was the Jewish Sabbath, and it was contrary to the customs of the Jews to leave anyone hanging on the cross on the Sabbath day; and that they might be certain that they were dead before removing them, the soldiers went up to them and broke the legs of the two thieves, but seeing that Jesus was already dead, they did not break any of his bones. One of the soldiers pierced his side with a spear, and blood and water flowed from the wound; and all this was done that the scriptures might be fulfilled, "*A*

76 Eliza R. Snow

bone of him shall not be broken," and *"They shall look on him whom they pierced."*

Joseph of Arimathea, a good man who loved Jesus, went to Pilate, the governor, and begged the body of Jesus; and when he had taken it down from the cross, he wrapped it in clean white linen and laid it in a new tomb of his, which had been hewn out of a rock, in which no body had ever been placed.

This tomb or sepulcher was in a garden, and it was near Mount Calvary on which Jesus was crucified, and many men and women who had followed after him when he was led to the cross went to the tomb and saw where his body was laid. And they rolled a large stone to the door of the tomb.

Some of the chief priests and Pharisees went to Pilate and told him that they remembered hearing that deceiver (as they called Jesus), when he was alive, say that after three days he would rise again; and they desired him to see that the sepulcher should be well secured until the third day, lest the disciples of Jesus should steal the body and circulate a report that he had arisen from the dead. And Pilate told them to set a watch and make it sure, and they went and put a seal on the stone which was at the door of the tomb and placed a body of soldiers to guard the place.

Early in the morning of the first day of the week (Sunday), long before the sun arose, Mary Magdalene went to visit the sepulcher of Jesus. To her great surprise, she found the stone rolled from the door of the tomb, and the body of Jesus was not there. With a sorrowful heart, Mary ran and told Peter and John that they had taken the Lord away, and she did not know where. And Peter and John ran to the sepulcher and went in and saw the linen clothes as Jesus had left them—the napkin that was about his head lying apart from the clothing of his body—and then Peter and John returned to their homes. But Mary stood there weeping; and looking into the sepulcher, she saw two angels clothed in white, one at the head, and the other at the feet, where the body of Jesus had lain. One of the angels asked her why she wept. She told them that she wept because they had taken the Lord away and she did not know where he was. She then turned around and saw Jesus

standing, and did not know that it was Jesus, but supposed him to be the gardener. Jesus said to her, "Why weepest thou? And whom seekest thou?" Mary said to him, "Sir, if thou hast borne him hence, tell me where thou hast laid him." Jesus then said, "Mary," and she knew him, and then she also knew that he had arisen from the dead, and her joy was full. There was a great earthquake at the time that Jesus arose—the angels of God came from heaven and removed the stone from the sepulcher, and at their appearance, the soldiers were frightened and fell to the ground and were like dead men. As soon as they had recovered from the terrible shock, some of them went into the city and reported what had happened, and the chief priests and the elders assembled, and when they had counseled together, they bribed the soldiers by giving them large sums of money, so that they, instead of telling the truth, reported that while they slept, his disciples came and stole the body away. And the chief priests promised to shield the soldiers from punishment.

And Jesus said to her, "Touch me not, for I am not yet ascended to my Father. But go to my brethren and say to them, 'I ascend to my Father and your Father, and to my God and your God.'" And Mary went and told the Apostles that she had seen the Lord, and repeated to them the words he had spoken to her.

Chapter 12

NOTHING could exceed the joy and astonishment of the Apostles and the other friends of Jesus when they were convinced that he had really arisen from the dead. Had they comprehended his sayings previous to his death, his resurrection would have been no surprise to them; but thinking that he had come to reign, temporally, a king over the people of Israel, every hope and expectation of their hearts were blasted when they saw him expire on the cross. They saw nothing before them but grief and mortification—their minds were filled with darkness and their souls with sorrow.

Oh, what a sad world this would have been to all of us if Jesus had not come forth from that sepulcher! If he had not been resurrected, we could never be, and the blessed assurance of a glorious resurrection to life and immortality beyond the grave would not, as it does now, animate our bosoms. With all the triumphant joy that these ancient Saints and Apostles felt when Jesus manifested himself to them from time to time

after he arose; we, the Latter-day Saints, are just as much interested in his resurrection as they were. Jesus, in dying and rising again, conquered death, and now it is not anything that a Saint ever need to fear.

That same evening after Jesus was resurrected, when all of the Apostles except Thomas were assembled with the doors of the house all closed for fear of the Jews, all of a sudden Jesus stood in the midst of them and said, "Peace be unto you," and to prove that it was really him, he showed his hands and his side which had the marks of the wounds he received when he was crucified. The Apostles were almost overcome with joy, and after Jesus left them, they hastened to Thomas and told him that they had actually seen the Lord. But it seemed too good for Thomas to believe, and he said that he would not believe unless he should see in the hands of Jesus, the print of the nails, and put his finger into them and thrust his hand into his side where the soldier pierced him with a spear.

Not many days after, all of the Apostles were together as before, and Jesus stood in their midst again, and, seeing

Thomas, he told him to put his finger into the prints in his hands and to reach out his hand and put it into his side and be no longer faithless, but believing. Thomas knew Jesus and exclaimed, "My Lord and my God."

At one time when some of Jesus' disciples were walking to a village not far from Jerusalem and were conversing about the strange things that had happened, Jesus came up and walked along in company with them. But they did not know him. He asked them why they were so sad and what it was that they were conversing about; and one of them asked him if he was a stranger and did not know what had happened. They then told how Jesus, a mighty prophet, had been falsely accused and put to death and how disappointed they felt because of his death. And they told him of the strange reports about his resurrection.

Then Jesus began with Moses and explained the sayings of all the prophets and instructed them that Jesus must die and rise again and taught them many things concerning himself, which they had never before understood. And when they

came to the village, they invited him to stop overnight with them, and they never thought who he was until they sat at the supper table, and he took the bread and blessed it and gave to them. Then their eyes were opened to know him, and he immediately vanished out of their sight.

On many occasions and in a variety of places, Jesus met with his friends and very kindly sought to remove their fears and unbelief by giving such simple proofs as they could naturally understand. When they thought him only a spirit, he told them to handle him and feel that he had flesh and bones; and at other times he ate in their presence and once, even broiled on coals, the fish which he ate. He gave them much instruction, and their understandings gradually were enlightened, and they began to comprehend the gospel more perfectly and for what purpose Jesus came into the world.

After telling his Apostles that all power and authority in heaven and on earth was given unto him, Jesus commissioned them to go into all the world and preach the gospel to every people but commanded them to tarry in Jerusalem until they were endowed with power from on high. As they were standing together on the Mount of Olives, Jesus ascended towards heaven, and a cloud hid him from their sight. And two angels clothed in white appeared to them and asked them why they stood gazing up into heaven and told them that the same Jesus should, in the last days, descend in the same manner as they had seen him ascend.

Chapter 13

WHEN instructing his followers, Jesus frequently called himself the shepherd and those who received his teachings, the sheep. At one time, he said to his disciples, "Other sheep I have who are not of this fold." Jesus was alluding to a people who, at that very time, were living on this western continent, but his disciples did not know what he meant, for they were entirely ignorant of any people except those on what we call the Eastern Hemisphere. If they had asked Jesus, he probably would have told them, but they did not ask.

The last words of Jesus in praying to his Father were, as he hung upon the cross, "Receive my spirit," and after his spirit left the body, he went immediately to his Father. His Father did receive him to His bosom, and no human heart in this state of mortality is capable of fully appreciating the transcendent joy of that glorious meeting of Father and Son. The Son had done the work that was given him to do, and the Father was satisfied.

During the three days that the body of Jesus lay in the tomb, he was not idle. Then it was that he went and preached to the spirits in prison—the spirits of people who had lived on the earth who had been rebellious and had died without obeying the gospel. Jesus went and preached the gospel to them, and those that received it could, according to the order of the gospel, be baptized by some of the Saints who were then living in the flesh. It is on the same principle that some of the Latter-day Saints have been baptized for the dead. The Apostle Paul, in writing to some of the ancient Saints who got into darkness and doubted whether there would be any resurrection, said, "Then why are we baptized for the dead if the dead rise not?"

At the period of time when Jesus lived and died and was resurrected on the eastern continent, the people of that country had no knowledge of the Western Hemisphere containing the continent of America.

Although on this portion of the earth the garden of Eden was planted, where Adam and Eve, our first parents, were

...in his hands, and ...again
...the mount, and ...
...Lord, thou hast ...
be encompassed about by the ...
Now behold, O Lord, and do ...
be ...
"angry with thy servant ...
use of his weakness before thee; ...
we know that thou art holy and ...
dwell in the heavens, and that ...
are "unworthy before thee; be- ...
use of the "fall our "natures have ...
become evil continually; neverthe- ...
s, O Lord, thou hast given us a ...
mandment that we must call ...
on thee, that from thee we may ...
ceive according to our desires. ...
Behold, O Lord, thou hast smit- ...
en us because of our iniquity, and ...
ast driven us forth, and for these ...
many years we have been in the ...
wilderness; nevertheless, thou hast ...
been "merciful unto us. O Lord, look ...
upon me in pity, and turn away ...
thine anger from this thy people, ...
and suffer not that they shall go ...

And the ...
eyes of the ...
saw the finger of ...
was as the finger of ...
flesh and blood; and ...
Jared "fell down before ...
for he was struck with ...

7 And the Lord ...
brother of Jared had ...
earth; and the Lord ...
Arise, why hast thou ...
8 And he saith ...
saw the finger of the ...
I feared lest he should ...
for I knew not that the ...
flesh and blood.
9 And the Lord said ...
Because of thy faith thou ...
that I shall take upon me ...
blood; and never has ...
before me with "such exceeding ...
as thou hast; for were it ...

placed when they came to colonize the world in the morning of its creation; through the many changes that had taken place, the earth had been divided—the two continents had been separated, and a mighty ocean was flowing between them.

We read in the Bible that the earth was divided in the days of Peleg, which was several generations before the day of Abraham. But we have no knowledge of the circumstances which occasioned the separation. We learn from the ancient prophets, as recorded in the Bible, that in the last days, these continents will be again united, and the water which now separates them will be turned back into the north.

The Book of Mormon gives us histories of people at different periods inhabiting this country, who, while they lived in the fear of the Lord and worked righteousness, were greatly blessed, and when they turned away from Him and went into iniquity were punished with wars and pestilences and, in some instances, utterly destroyed. The descendants of Lehi, who came from Jerusalem six hundred years before the birth of Jesus, were the inhabitants of this western country at the time of his birth. They brought the records of their fathers containing the words of the ancient prophets who foretold the coming of Jesus to die for the redemption of the world; and when they kept the commandments of God, He spoke to them and instructed them through prophets and inspired men in their midst. These prophets, who were greatly beloved and respected by the good, were hated, persecuted, and held in derision by the wicked; and when they boldly declared the truths of God and called on the people to repent, the wicked were so enraged that the prophets were often obliged to flee from place to place for the preservation of their lives.

As the time drew near when Jesus was to be born, it seemed that Satan exerted all his power to stir up the hearts of the people to madness against the prophets whom God inspired to testify of it and against all those who believed their words. There was one prophet by the name of Samuel, a Lamanite, who was commanded to warn the inhabitants of the city Zarahemla of the awful judgments that would be poured out upon them if they did not speedily repent.

Chapter 14

SAMUEL prophesied of the coming of Jesus, that the time was near at hand when he would be born. He also gave the people a strange sign by which they might know the time of his birth, which was that the night before Jesus was born would be as light as the day, so that there would be two days and a night in which there would be no darkness; and Samuel the prophet told them about the length of time that would elapse before this sign would appear. He also said that at that time, a new star, which had never been seen before, should make its appearance; and other signs also should be seen in the heavens.

He told the people if they would repent of their sins and believe in the name of Jesus, they should be saved from the awful destructions that would surely come upon the wicked; for, he said to them, Jesus will be crucified, and at the time of his death there will be lightening and earthquakes, and many fierce and terrible judgments will be poured out upon those

who disbelieve the words of the prophets and continue in their wickedness.

At that time, the people of the great city Zarahemla were so wicked that they would not allow the prophets of God to enter their gates, and the only way that Samuel could approach them so as to warn them of their impending danger was to stand upon the wall and there proclaim with a loud voice what the Lord commanded him to say. While in that position, many threw stones to kill him as he stood preaching to the people, but the angels of heaven were there for his protection, and the wicked could not destroy him. Those that believed came out of the city and were baptized in the name of Jesus for the remission of their sins and joined themselves to those who feared the Lord and were obedient to the words of the prophets.

As the time approached when Samuel had predicted that the sign concerning the birth of Jesus should appear, the wicked began to exult and say that the time had expired and the prophecies were all false; and they ridiculed those that believed in them and threatened to put them to death and had appointed a day when they would destroy every one of them, if the sign was not to be seen before that day arrived.

There was a very good man called Nephi, who trusted in God and believed in the coming of Jesus; he went out alone, and, bowing down, he prayed fervently for his friends and brethren who were in danger of being destroyed by their enemies. And while he was praying, a voice came to him saying that the sign should be given that very night, and on the next day Jesus should be born. It was the voice of the Lord speaking to Nephi; and Nephi rejoiced exceedingly when he heard the voice, for he knew that the words were true, and his sorrow and mourning were turned into joy and thanksgiving; and he wept and told the good news to his brethren.

That same evening, the sun went down as usual, but no darkness followed the setting of the sun, but the nighttime was as light as the day. Instead of the wicked slaying the righteous, great fear fell upon the unbelievers when they saw the sign that had been foretold, and many of them fell to the

ground as if they were dead. It was the same in all the land, east, west, north and south; and all the people saw the long day and witnessed the appearance of a new star; and all things were fulfilled which the prophets had spoken concerning that time.

No tongue can express the feelings of joy that filled the hearts of the prophets and of all who believed on them, when they knew not only by miraculous signs but, by the unerring testimony of the spirit of God, that Jesus the Messiah, the Savior of the world, had really taken a mortal body and had come to redeem the fallen children of Adam. It was true, he was a long distance off, and they were separated by a mighty ocean, but they knew that he had come and that all people on the face of the earth were interested in his coming.

During the thirty-three years and upwards of the lifetime of Jesus, we have no account of his manifesting himself to those who believed in him, that lived on the western continent, but in all that time, there were many who were inspired by the Spirit of God who went forth testifying of the truths of salvation and teaching the principles of righteousness and a belief in a judgment to come. And in every land they were more or less persecuted, and from time to time they were hunted and driven. Yet they had seasons of peace and prosperity—when the people listened to the teachings of the inspired men, as many did for a few years after the birth of Jesus. Their peace and prosperity was great, but it was not long until the most part turned away and went into sin, and at the time of the death of Jesus, there was much division and strife throughout the land, but those that did believe in him were clothed with the power of God and performed great miracles, even to the raising of the dead to life.

Chapter 15

THE prophets had foretold that at the time of the crucifixion of Jesus, there should be darkness on the Western Continent for three days and nights. Although many great and wonderful miracles had been performed by those that believed and lived in obedience to the words of the prophets, many began to doubt and say that the prophets had spoken falsely.

On the very day and at the very hour when Jesus, the Son of God, was nailed to a cross, there arose a most fearful storm here in the land of America; although it was not called America then, for at that time it was inhabited by the people called Nephites and Lamanites. That storm was the most fearful one that ever was known. The wind blew in hurricanes and tempests, while the flashes of lightning and the awful peals of thunder were fearfully terrific.

In the midst of the dreadful scene, the great city Zarahemla took fire and was burned to ashes. It was in this same city where, before the birth of Jesus, the prophet Samuel tried to preach, but the people would not suffer him to remain in the city, but drove him out, and he got upon the walls and stood and warned them of the judgments of God that would come upon them if they did not repent.

Very many other cities were destroyed—some were burned—some were sunk and some buried in the depths of the sea—some were taken up by tremendous whirlwinds, while others were shaken by earthquakes until the buildings fell and crushed the inhabitants. In some places, the rocks were torn asunder and thrown up in huge mountainous piles, while in other parts they were scattered about in broken fragments.

This awful scene lasted three hours, the same length of time that Jesus hung in agony on the cross—and in the short space of three hours, the whole face of this western continent was fearfully changed. Of the many once-flourishing cities, both in the north and south, a few remained, but those few were very much injured by the tempests and earthquakes, and many of the inhabitants perished.

When the storm ceased, the whole land was covered with darkness; and the darkness was so dense that the people that outlived the storm could feel the vapor of darkness. It was impossible for them to make any light whatever—they could neither light candles nor kindle very dry wood so as to make even a glimmer of light; and there was not the least ray to be seen from the sun, moon, or stars.

This was a dreadful state for the people to remain in after the awful calamities which had come upon them. The darkness lasted during the time of three days and nights. And there was great weeping, mourning, and lamentation among the people who had been warned of the things that were coming upon the earth and had been called upon to repent of their sins and turn to the Lord. When it was too late, they saw their folly and bewailed their wretched condition. And in many places, they filled the air with their cries and lamentations that they had not forsaken their sins before those calamities overtook them so that they might have been spared with their sons and daughters to enjoy their society.

Then the sound of a voice went forth over all the land, and it was heard by all the living that were spared from the awful scourge. The voice was the voice of Jesus, and he spoke to all the inhabitants of the earth. He reproved the people for their sins and told them how they had persecuted those who had sought to do them good and that, in consequence of their wickedness, all these calamities had come upon them, and those who were the greatest sinners had been utterly destroyed as the prophets had predicted.

The voice then said, "O all you that are spared because you were more righteous than they; will you not now turn unto me and repent of your sins and be converted that I may heal you? Yea, verily I say unto you, if ye will come unto me, ye shall have eternal life. Behold, my arm of mercy is extended towards you, and whosoever will come, I will receive; and blessed are they that come unto me. Behold, I am Jesus Christ, the Son of God. And as many as have received me, to them have I given power to become the sons of God; and even so will I to as many as shall believe on my name; for, by me redemption cometh, and in me is the law of Moses fulfilled. I am the light and the life of the world. I have laid down my life and have taken it up again: therefore, repent and come unto me, ye ends of the earth, and be ye saved."

Chapter 16

AFTER three days, the fearful darkness passed away. The terrible earthquakes also ceased so that the earth did not shake and tremble, and the frightful sounds caused by the rending of the rocks were no longer heard, and the great chasms that had been made in the ground closed up; and then the weeping and lamentations of the people were turned into praise and thanksgiving to Jesus their Redeemer.

The people that were left alive were not the most wicked class of society—they were such as had never stoned the prophets, and they had never been guilty of shedding the blood of the saints, while those who had been guilty of all manner of wickedness and had been filled with the spirit of persecution, had some of them been sunk and buried in the earth—some were drowned—some were burned with fire—some were crushed to death by the fall of buildings—some were carried away and dashed to pieces by whirlwinds, while others were destroyed by the suffocating vapor which accompanied the thick darkness.

After these marvelous things had transpired and all those that were spared, both of the Nephites and the Lamanites, had humbled themselves before God and repented of all their sins, they were greatly blessed—they were united together and were filled with the spirit of God. Their union was so great and their faith in Jesus so perfect that he manifested himself to them but not till after he had ascended into heaven at Jerusalem at the time when he stood on the Mount of Olives with some of his disciples. And it will be recollected that as he ascended, a cloud received him out of their sight, and the angels of God appeared to those who saw him ascend and asked them why they stood gazing up into heaven and told them that the time would come when he would descend in the same way that they had seen him ascend. This prophecy of the angels will be fulfilled in these last days.

In the land which was called Bountiful, there was a temple which was not destroyed by any of the convulsions of the earth at the time when Jesus was crucified. A great multitude of people had gathered around the temple and were conversing

one with another about the wonderful changes that had taken place, when they heard the sound of a voice as if it came out of heaven; and with great astonishment every eye was turned to see, if possible, from whence the sound proceeded, but they did not understand the voice. It was neither harsh nor loud, but it seemed to pierce their very souls and caused their hearts to burn and their whole frames to tremble. And they heard it the second time, and still they did not understand it; and while, with the utmost anxiety, they were steadfastly looking towards heaven from whence it seemed to come, they heard it the third time, and then they understood it, and it said to them, "Behold my beloved Son, in whom I am well pleased—in whom I have glorified my name, hear ye him."

The people then saw a man coming down from heaven, clothed in a white robe, and he came and stood in their midst, and the eyes of the whole multitude were fastened upon him—no one spoke, for they were all filled with surprise, not knowing what it meant, but thought that an angel had appeared unto them. But it was Jesus—he had come to bless and comfort them. And he stretched forth his hand and said, "I am Jesus Christ, whom the prophets testified should come into the world; and behold, I am the light and the life of the world; and I have drank out of the bitter cup which the Father hath given me and have glorified the Father in taking upon me the sins of the world, in which I have suffered the will of the Father, in all things, from the beginning."

When the multitude heard this, they all fell to the earth, remembering that it had been foretold by their prophets that Jesus should visit them and show himself unto them after he arose from the dead and had ascended to heaven.

Then Jesus told them to rise up and come to him and put their hands into his side, and feel the prints of the nails in his hands and feet, and know for themselves that it was really Jesus, of whom the prophets had written. Filled with joy and gladness, the whole multitude shouted aloud, "Hosanna! Blessed be the name of the Most High God!" And they fell down at the feet of Jesus and worshiped him.

Chapter 17

WHAT an auspicious time—what a strange and interesting event! Jesus, the Son of God, the Savior of the world, who had been crucified at Jerusalem, had been to preach to the spirits in prison, had returned and, with his body resurrected from the tomb, had ascended up to heaven, had now again descended on the Western Continent and was standing in the presence of a multitude of people who saw him and heard his voice. It is no wonder that when they understood who he was, that in joyful astonishment they should have fallen to the earth.

There was a man by the name of Nephi, whom Jesus commanded to arise and come forward. And he arose and went and bowed himself before Jesus and kissed his feet. Jesus told him to arise, and he stood up, and Jesus gave him authority to baptize in His name for the remission of sins. He also called eleven others unto him and conferred on them the same authority and gave them the same instructions as he gave to his chosen disciples in Jerusalem. Jesus stood talking

for a long time, sometimes addressing himself to the twelve he had chosen, and at other times to the multitude, instructing them how to be saved by being baptized in His name for the remission of their sins and then by keeping all of His commandments. With very many other things, he told the twelve that they were a light to the people who were called a remnant of the house of Joseph and that this was the land of their inheritance, which the Father had given unto them.

When Jesus looked upon the multitude and saw that they were not able to comprehend all the words that his Father had commissioned him to say to them, he told them to return to their homes and ponder what he had said to them and ask the Father in his name that they might understand and thus prepare their minds for the morrow, when he would visit them again. He told them that he must return to the Father and then go and show himself to the lost tribes of the house of Israel and come back to them next day. Jesus was not idle—he was constantly doing good.

When the people saw that Jesus was going to leave them, they looked so sorrowful and expressed in their countenances so much desire that he should remain longer, that his heart was filled with sympathy, and he told them to bring all of the sick, blind, lame, deaf, and all that were afflicted with any kind of disease, that he might do for them the same as he had done for their brethren in Jerusalem. And the whole multitude went immediately and brought the blind, the deaf, and dumb, and all that were in any way afflicted, and he healed every one. And all those who had been healed, and all those that were whole, bowed down and worshipped him, and as many as could get near enough kissed his feet and bathed them with tears.

Then Jesus commanded them to bring their little children; and they brought them and sat them down on the ground around him, and he stood in the midst of the children, for the multitude of people drew back and gave place for them so that all could be brought. As the group of children sat there, Jesus told the people to kneel down—he also knelt and prayed

mightily to his Father, and the Holy Spirit rested down on the whole multitude, and they were filled with greater joy than it is possible to express. And when Jesus had done praying, he arose and told the people to arise from their knees, and he blessed them and said they were blessed because of their faith; and he wept, saying, "My joy is full." And he took the little children, one by one, and blessed them and prayed for them. And again he wept and said to the multitude, "Behold your little ones."

And the people looked and saw the heavens opened and the angels of God descending in the midst of fire; and they came down and encircled the children around, and those little ones were encircled about with fire, and the angels ministered unto them. And the whole multitude heard, and they all saw the beautiful, grand, and heavenly sight. It was a most splendid tableau for most eyes to gaze upon. It was exhibited in the presence of about two thousand and five hundred persons—men, women, and children.

After this glorious exhibition, Jesus commanded the twelve whom he had chosen to bring bread and wine to him, and while they were gone for the bread and wine, he told the multitude to sit down on the ground. And he took the bread and blessed it and gave to his disciples and told them to eat and then give to the multitude, and administered the wine in the same manner, after which he gave them a great deal of instruction. And then, one by one, he touched his disciples whom he had chosen and gave them power to impart the Holy Ghost. After he had touched them all, a cloud overshadowed the multitude so that they could not see Jesus, and he departed from them and ascended into heaven.

Then every man took his wife and children and went to his own home.

Chapter 18

AS the people returned to their homes, they spread the word abroad to a great distance that Jesus had appeared and ministered to them and that he was coming again on the morrow. The excitement was very great, and the people were so anxious to be present next day that many toiled and traveled all night, lest they should be belated and not be in time at the place appointed when Jesus should make his appearance; and when a great multitude had come together, Nephi and the rest of the twelve disciples whom Jesus had chosen went and stood in the midst of the people.

The multitude of people assembled was so large that Nephi and his brethren divided them into twelve separate bodies, and the twelve Apostles prayed in their midst, after which they all arose. And the Apostles instructed the assemblies of people by repeating word for word what Jesus had spoken to them on the preceding day. Then, again, they knelt and prayed to the Father in the name of Jesus, that the Holy Ghost might be given unto them.

When they arose, the whole multitude followed the Twelve Apostles to the water; and Nephi went down into it and was baptized, and after he had come out of the water, the Holy Ghost fell upon them, and they were filled with the Holy Ghost and with fire. And the appearance of fire came down from heaven in the sight of the whole multitude, and it encircled the Twelve Apostles around, and angels came out of heaven and ministered to them. And while the angels were ministering to them, Jesus also came and stood in their midst.

What a glorious scene for mortal eyes to behold! Let us pause a moment and reflect on the wonderful grandeur of this interesting spectacle as it was then presented to the view of the astonished multitude. Jesus, the Son of God, who had died to redeem the world, had been resurrected and had ascended on high, stood there in the presence of that vast assemblage of people, with Twelve Apostles whom he had chosen to preach the gospel of life and salvation on the western continent, all encircled in flame, and forming one of the grandest and most beautiful of tableaux ever gazed upon by an earthly audience.

Jesus then spoke to the multitude and commanded all to kneel down upon the earth, and he commanded his disciples to pray, and when they commenced to pray, they prayed unto Jesus and called him their Lord and their God.

And Jesus went a short distance from them and bowed himself to the earth and gave thanks to his Father that He had given the Holy Ghost unto his chosen ones, and he prayed for them and also for all those who should believe in him through their words. And when he returned to his disciples, he blest them, and as he smiled upon them, the light of his countenance fell upon them, and they became as white as the countenance and as the garments of Jesus, which were beautifully white, above all earthly whiteness.

On that occasion, the manifestations were great and marvelous—they could not be written, and Jesus told them it was in consequence of their great faith, which was greater than he saw at any time among the Jews at Jerusalem, where none had seen and heard as great things as were shown to them.

Then, although there had been none brought, Jesus took bread and wine, and after he had blest it he gave to his disciples, and they gave it to that great multitude. And when they had all eaten and drank, they were filled with the spirit of God and gave glory to Jesus, whom they both saw and heard. And he said, "Behold, now I finish the commandment which the Father hath commanded concerning this people, which are a remnant of the house of Israel." Jesus also taught the little children and loosed their tongues, and they spoke great and marvelous things, even greater than had been revealed to their fathers. And he healed all that were sick, lame, blind, and deaf and also manifested his power by raising the dead.

He explained many of the words of the prophets recorded in the Old Testament and commanded the people to read them, that they might understand what God had purposed concerning the inhabitants of the earth. And he foretold all things from that time until he should come in his glory, "even until the elements should melt with fervent heat, and the earth should be wrapped together as a scroll, and the heavens

and the earth shall pass away"—when all kindreds, nations, and tongues shall stand before God and be judged of their works.

So great was the power of God poured out upon the people that the next day after Jesus had appeared in their midst the second time, they came together; and they heard and saw the little children, even babes, open their mouths and speak marvelous things, which they were forbidden to write. And from that time, the disciples began to baptize and teach in the name of Jesus all that came to them. And Jesus often showed himself to them and often broke bread and blest it and gave to them, which he commanded them and all his Saints to do in remembrance of him until he comes.

These are the last days, and God is now preparing a people, even The Church of Jesus Christ of Latter-day Saints, that they may be pure enough to receive Jesus and abide his presence at his coming.

About the Authors

Eliza R. Snow

Eliza Roxcy Snow, born January 21, 1804, was one of the most prominent women in the early days of the LDS Church. She was hired to teach the Prophet Joseph Smith's children and through time became well acquainted with him.

Eliza was the first secretary of the LDS Women's Relief Society. She was well known for her poetry, many of which became songs for the LDS Hymn book. They called her Zion's Poetess. She died December 5, 1887.

Kathleen Barlow

Kathleen Barlow is the mother of twelve children. She has taught home school for twenty years. She is currently interested in republishing moral, character building, and Christian titles for children and adults.

0 26575 59407 2